# THE BREAD MACHINE COOKBOOK

## donna rathmell german

TAYLOR TRADE PUBLISHING

The Bread Machine Cookbook, a nitty gritty® Cookbook

©2013 by Taylor Trade Publishing
An imprint of
The Rowman & Littlefield Publishing Group, Inc.
4501 Forbes Boulevard, Suite 200
Lanham, MD 20706
www.rowman.com

Produced by CulinartMedia, Inc.
Design: Harrah Lord
Layout: Patty Holden
Editor: Susan Stover
Photography: Eising Food Photography (all rights reserved)
www.culinartmedia.com

Distributed by National Book Network
1-800-462-6420

ISBN 978-1-58979-884-7
Library of Congress Cataloguing-in-Publication Data on file

Printed in China

# CONTENTS

# THE BASICS

This book includes new variations on favorite recipes, new recipes and additional information on how to use your bread machine and the bread to the fullest extent possible. If you are like some bread machine owners, you may use the machine frequently for a few months and then put it away or not use it, then take it out again. Or, you may only use it during fall or winter. The additional section "Getting the most from your machine," is designed to give you new ideas and make the machine work for you. After all, man does not live by bread alone…

## ABOUT BREAD MACHINES

It is important for you to become familiar with the owner's manual and/or the recipe book that came with your machine. There are a few pieces of information to know about your particular machine in order to make any recipe.

## INGREDIENT ORDER

Manufacturers indicate the order in which the ingredients should be put into the pan. In most machines, you start with the liquid; in a few, you begin with yeast and then flour. The really important point is that the liquid ingredients are kept away from the yeast until the machine starts.

## RECIPE SIZE FOR YOUR MACHINE

You must determine the size of your machine. If your machine manual does not specify the size of the machine given by weight of loaf, it is easily determined by looking at the amount of flour or flour equivalents in the recipes that come with the machine.

In general, 1 lb. machines use 2 to 2¼ cups of bread flour or 2 to 2¾ total cups of combined flours such as bread flour, whole wheat, rye, oats, corn, etc. For whole grain flours, 2½ to 3 cups may be used. If you have a 1 lb. machine, you will use the Small recipe, depending on the ingredients and flour equivalents.

A 1½ lb. machine uses 3 cups of bread flour or 3½ to 4 total cups of combined flours such as bread flour, whole wheat, rye, oats, corn, etc. Up to 5 cups of whole grain flours may be used in most 1½ lb. machines without fear of overflows. Most 1½ lb. machines will take the Medium recipe, depending on the ingredients and flour equivalents.

A full 2 lb. machine can use up to 4 cups of bread flour, although I find that 3½ cups usually results in a nice loaf of bread at or just over the lip of the pan. A total of 4 to 5 cups of combination flours (bread with whole wheat, oats, rye, corn, etc.) may easily be used and up to 6 cups of whole-grain flours. Some machines are being introduced as 2 lb. machines, but the size of the pan is the same as the 1½ lb. pan, and therefore must use Medium size recipes. It is necessary to keep an eye on the dough to prevent overflows. A full 2 lb. machine will use the Large recipe.

After years of working with all machine makes and models, I can assure you that there are some variables and individual preferences in the sizes of recipes used. For example, one friend with a lb. machine (2 cups of flour, generally) makes Medium recipes, which would seem too large for her machine. My father, however, has a large machine and consistently uses recipes with just 2 cups of flour; in the identical machine I use 3½ cups of flour.

Unlike any other bread machine cookbook on the market, I give you three different sizes for each recipe. If a recipe is too large, next time use a smaller size. Most machines can make a smaller size recipe.

**A few words about pushing the maximum flour capacity of your bread machine:** if at any time it sounds like the machine is struggling with a large amount of flour, add a tablespoon or two of water (or more if necessary) to soften the dough. If the machine is struggling, it could cause damage to the motor.

The sides of the machine may require scraping to help get all ingredients to the kneading paddle. Once the dough has formed a ball it will do just fine and may be left. If it has taken the machine a long time to knead the ingredients into a ball, you can stop the machine and start it over from the beginning, giving the dough a little longer knead.

One of the main concerns about using too much flour is overflowing the sides of the pan. Usually you will end up with a mushroom—the dough may cook onto the lid of the pan or may not cook properly at the top. The real mess, however, is when the dough spills down the sides of the pan into the inside of the machine and onto the heating elements. Cleanup is a messy, time-consuming chore. It is difficult to remove all dough from the heating elements, but it burns off the next time the machine is used.

It is wise to check the dough during the second rise. If it looks too high, use a bamboo skewer and pierce deep into the dough to deflate it. Do not use metal objects that could scratch the pan. If you have absolutely used the wrong size recipe and it is starting to overflow, remove a portion of the dough. This enables you to at least salvage something!

## BREAD MACHINE CYCLES

Initially, all recipes were tested using only the basic white cycles. Later testing has indicated that some machines perform more consistently on the sweet cycle.

The same cycle may have many names. A sweet cycle may also be called mix, or fruit and nut. Most machines now have whole wheat cycles, but any machine can make whole wheat bread on the regular (basic, white) cycle.

Add ingredients, like raisins, at the beginning of the second kneading, or during the rest between kneadings. If you have only one kneading, add extra ingredients as soon as dough has formed a ball, about 5 to 10 minutes into the kneading.

Basic white bread cycles may have one or two main kneadings depending on the machine. Some machines have only a basic cycle, which is used for all breads. Sweet cycles should be used with recipes containing 2 tablespoons or more sugar and/or fat (butter, margarine or oil). These cycles may have a longer rising time. The baking temperature is lower than the basic cycles for the higher sugar content of the breads. French bread cycles may or may not have a longer rising time but all have a higher baking temperature to crisp the crust.

Raisin cycles have a beep to indicate when to add raisins, nuts or other similar ingredients. Generally the beep is about 5 minutes before the end of the kneading. The cycles may have a lower baking temperature (like the sweet cycle).

Whole grain cycles generally have longer kneading and rising cycles.

Dough cycles include the initial kneading of the dough and one rise, after which time the dough is removed from the machine, shaped, allowed to rise and baked in a conventional oven. This is the cycle used for bagels, rolls, pizza crust, etc. For best results, some machines should be stopped after the first rise and before the second kneading.

## OTHER FEATURES

Timers and digital controls enable the user to place ingredients in the machine and to tell it when to have the bread ready. Some machines even have a dough cycle timer that is great for things like pizza or breakfast dough. Recipes containing ingredients that could spoil if unrefrigerated (eggs, milk, cheese, etc.) should not be used with the timer. As a general rule, only use a timer on recipes that you have previously made and with which you are comfortable. Preheating periods are found on some machines. Basically the machine heats all ingredients to the proper temperature prior to starting the kneading period.

Crust controls are usually buttons pushed when you start your machine, such as basic white, light setting. Some machines have a control knob. The controls shorten or lengthen the baking time by about 5 minutes.

Power outage protection prevents a short (usually 10 minutes or less) loss of electricity from stopping the entire machine process. If this is not included with your machine and you have a loss of electricity, simply remove the dough and finish baking the bread conventionally.

Viewing windows are a nice feature if you like to frequently check the process of your bread. It is always a good idea to check the dough about 5 minutes into the initial kneading to make sure that all is going well. If you don't have a viewing window, simply open the lid long enough to check the dough. Don't leave the machine open for long periods of time.

## BREAD INGREDIENTS
### YEAST
A living plant, yeast eats sugar and produces carbon dioxide which, in turn, mixes with gluten in flour to make the dough rise. Without yeast the bread will be a flat, unleavened bread. Both active dry and fast-acting yeasts may be purchased either in envelopes (1 envelope equals approximately 2¼ teaspoon) or in bulk. It is much cheaper to buy yeast in bulk in a jar or vacuum packed.

In recent yeast testing, the fast-acting yeast (sometimes called rapid or quick) consistently resulted in loaves that rose higher than those made with the regular dry active yeast.

Yeast responds to ambient temperatures. It may be necessary to increase yeast in colder weather or to decrease it in very hot temperatures. Too much yeast may cause air pockets or air bubbles. Compressed (cake) yeast is not recommended for use in bread machines.

### LIQUIDS
Liquid ingredients should be warmed to lukewarm for best performance. The

liquid should be warm or comfortable to the inside of your wrist—about 110°F.

Some ingredients such as fruits and cottage cheese may be difficult to knead into the dough. It is helpful to take a rubber spatula and scrape down the sides of the pan and push the ingredients toward the kneading paddle. Once the paddle has picked up all ingredients, let it knead by itself for about 5 minutes and then check the dough consistency again for a smooth dough ball. If the process has taken quite a long time, you may wish to turn off the machine and start it again. This gives the dough with the correct consistency a longer kneading. Because the moisture must be pulled out of bananas or potatoes or spinach it may require a longer period of kneading before a judgment can be made as to whether to add more liquid. If lumps of the fruit, cheese or vegetable are still visible, let it knead longer before adding water. Adding water too early may create a dough that is too moist. Should this happen, then you need to add flour, a tablespoon at a time, until a smooth ball of dough is obtained. Always use very ripe bananas for the best moisture content.

## FATS

In bread baking, fats provide flavor, make the bread moist and give it a soft crumb. Fats used include margarine, butter, vegetable oil, olive oil, shortening or lard. Butter or margarine need not be melted to be placed in the machine. Applesauce or apple and orange juice concentrates may be equally substituted for the liquid.

## SUGAR

A necessity in yeast bread baking, sugar feeds the yeast, enabling it to rise. In addition, it assists in the browning of the crust. Sugar substitutes for bread baking include white or brown sugar, barley malt syrup, honey, molasses, and maple syrup. Sugar substitutes, such as NutraSweet®, etc. should not be used since they break down during the heating process.

## SALT

A growth-inhibitor of the yeast, salt provides a counterbalance for the sugar and brings out the flavor of the bread. Reduce the amount of salt, if breads are not rising properly.

## EGGS

Eggs are sometimes used in bread baking to add richness, color, and flavor. One yolk or white may be used for ½ egg, which equals approximately 2 tablespoons liquid. One large egg equals approximately ¼ cup liquid.

## FLOUR

There are many different kinds of flours, grains or cereals, which may be used for structure in your bread baking. **White or bread flour should be at least 50 percent of the flour or grain used.** A higher percentage of whole-grain flour will result in a low, heavy, dense bread. Flours may be substituted cup for cup with other flours, grains or cereals.

Any grain with the entire hull, or outer lining intact, is called a groat, such as oats and buckwheat. Once the hulls are removed, the remaining kernel contains the bran, germ and endosperm. The bran and germ of any grain contain the majority of the nutrients. Up to 80 percent of the vitamins and minerals are lost by the grinding and refining of the grain into white flour (which consists of pure endosperm). Generally, darker flour; wheat, rye, rice, etc., has more of the germ and bran included and makes more nutritional bread. Flour containing the germ and/or bran should be refrigerated or stored in a dark, cool place.

In yeast breads, a wheat flour base, when kneaded, develops gluten. The gluten forms an elastic substance, which traps carbon dioxide released from the yeast. This is the key ingredient in the wheat which makes dough rise. Other flours with less gluten must be mixed with wheat flour to a maximum ratio of 1 to 1.

**Wheat** is the most common flour for bread baking. There are many varieties of wheat flours. Differences include where the wheat is grown, hard or soft, what section of the wheat kernel is used, or how the flour is milled.

**All-Purpose Flour** is a blend of hard and soft wheat that may be used for a variety of baking needs including breads and cakes. All-purpose loses many of its natural vitamins and nutrients during the milling process. "Enriched" flour replaces the nutrients iron, thiamine, riboflavin and niacin. Bleached all-purpose flour is chemically whitened; unbleached flour is allowed to whiten naturally.

**Bread Flour** is recommended for most of the recipes in this book. Bread flour, derived from hard wheat, is higher in protein and gluten. Bread flour produces a finer grain bread.

**Whole Wheat Flour** is milled from the entire wheat kernel, containing all the natural nutrients. It is lower in gluten than white flour and should not exceed

50 percent of the flour ingredients. Sometimes labeled as graham flour, in this book whole wheat flour is used for both types. Some mills label graham flour differently than whole wheat, if the graham contains 100 percent of the kernel and coarsely milled; while whole wheat may be cleaned and sifted.

**Gluten Flour/Gluten** is protein removed from wheat flour by rinsing off the starch. The protein is dried, ground and added to white flour. It is added in small amounts to low-gluten bread dough for a lighter texture.

**Wheat Germ** is the embryo of the wheat berry. A wonderful source of protein, fat, vitamins, and minerals, wheat germ gives bread a slightly nutty flavor. Add 1 tablespoon wheat germ per cup of flour. Store in the refrigerator.

**Wheat Berries** are high in protein and low in calories. The berries are wheat grain before any grinding or milling. Berries must be soaked, preferably overnight, prior to use. Store in a dry, cool place.

**Cracked Wheat** is crushed, toasted wheat berries. Cracked wheat must be soaked, preferably in the recipe liquid, a minimum of 1 hour prior to kneading.

**Wheat Bulgur** is parboiled, crushed and toasted wheat berries. It can be used interchangeably with cracked wheat, without soaking.

**Rolled Wheat Flakes**, similar to rolled oats, add a unique flavor and texture to bread.

**Barley Flour** has a very low gluten content and must be used with a high gluten flour. Barley has a mild nutty flavor.

**Barley Malt** gives bread a rich, grainy flavor. It is made by soaking whole barley grains, sprouting, drying, and grinding the grains. Barley malt, used in bread baking and beer making tastes similar to blackstrap molasses and the two may be used interchangeably.

**Cornmeal** is ground from whole corn kernels. Available as yellow, white or blue cornmeal, it is less nutritious than other grains.

**Rolled Oats** are oat grains, steamed, rolled into flakes, and dried, with the bran, germ, and nutrients intact. Fairly high in protein, oats are also high in vitamins B and E.

**Oat bran** is nutritious and adds fiber. In breads, oat bran adds moisture to the texture.

**Oat Flour** is milled or ground rolled oats. It can be made in a food processor or blender by blending 1 cup at a time at high speed until a fine flour forms, about 1 minute.

**White Rice** has the husk, bran, and germ removed, lessening its nutritional value. **Brown Rice** is the entire grain.

**Rice Flour** is a low-gluten flour combined with bread flour in bread making.

**Rice Bran** is the outer layer of the kernel and has high nutritional value.

**Rice Syrup** is a sweetener containing no fructose or sucrose.

**Rye Flour** is milled from the entire rye berry and has a high nutrient content. The darker the color, the stronger tasting and higher in nutrient value. There is less gluten in rye flours, so use it with white flour in bread making.

**Rye Meal** is a coarser grind of the rye kernel than flour.

**Rye Berry** or kernel of rye, as wheat berries, may be sprouted and used in its entirety in bread for the highest nutritional content.

**Soybeans** are a source of high protein, used in many different ways and foods.

**Soy Flakes** are pressed soybeans, added to bread for crunchy, tasty bread.

**Soy Flour** is high in protein and low in calories, added in small quantities to high protein breads. It adds moisture and is a natural preservative.

**Amaranth** is extremely high in protein, vitamins, minerals, and calcium. The grains are cooked for a hot cereal, sprouted for salads or breads, toasted as nuts, or even popped like popcorn.

**Buckwheat/Kasha** has a very high protein count. Nutritionally, it is rich in vitamins B and E and has a high calcium content. Buckwheat flour is commonly used in pancakes.

**Quinoa:** is extremely high in pro–tein, from 14 to 19 percent. It is also an excellent source of calcium and is high in lysine, as well as vitamin C, thiamine, riboflavin, and niacin. Quinoa grains may be cooked the same as rice. The flour is used in quinoa bread, which has a slightly nutty taste.

## IMPORTANT HINTS AND TROUBLESHOOTING

**1.** Read the owner's manual that came with the machine.

**2.** Read the introductory chapters of this book.

**3.** Measure the ingredients and put them into the pan in the order specified.

**4.** Choose the cycle and the setting.

**5.** Press the start button.

**6.** Check the dough after about 5 minutes of kneading to ensure that the dough has formed a round, smooth ball.

**7.** Remove the fully baked loaf of bread from the machine 2 to 4 hours later, depending on the machine.

**Perhaps the single most important thing to check is the consistency of the dough after 5 to 10 minutes of kneading.**

Look through the viewing window or open it briefly during the kneading process. Open it long enough to check the consistency and then to make any adjustments necessary. Don't leave the lid open long and don't open it during the baking cycle.

The flour and other ingredients pick up the moisture from the air. The moisture content of the grain berries may vary as will the absorbency of whole grain flour according to how it was milled. As a result, the dough may have too much liquid, which could result in an overflow or a sunken top.

When kneading dough by machine, you can see the right consistency. If you have problems with consistency, allow the machine to knead the dough for approximately 5 minutes and then look at the dough. With few exceptions, it should form a nice, smooth ball. Sometimes the ball will be round and other times, it may take on more of a cylindrical shape which "tornadoes" up the side of the pan.

By watching the dough on a regular basis, you will soon develop a sense for what looks right. If you stick your finger in and touch it, it should feel moist but not really be sticky. Dough that is too dry will not mix properly or it may cause the machine to struggle (you'll hear it). It may be uneven or have two or more balls of dough. In this case, add the liquid you are using, one tablespoon at a time, until the required consistency is reached. Conversely, too wet dough will not be able to form a ball, and flour should be added one tablespoon at a time until the required consistency is obtained.

If you hear the paddle rotating, but the ingredients on top of the dough are not moving—check to see that the paddle is inserted properly. Sometimes either the paddle was not placed on the kneading shaft correctly or it has slipped. The easiest way to check is to turn off the machine, reach in and feel whether the paddle is on correctly. It can usually just be pushed harder onto the shaft and the machine restarted without any difficulties.

If the bread rises well but then collapses during baking—it is either rising too fast in hot weather (cut yeast, sugar and/or increase salt or use a shorter cycle) or the size of the recipe is too large (use a smaller size recipe).

Too much moisture in the dough may cause a sunken top or a mushroom. Cut back the amount of liquid by ¼ cup and add it in slowly as the machine is kneading. Stop adding it when the dough forms a smooth round ball.

If the crust is too dark or brown —bake on "light" if your machine has crust control. If not, try removing the bread about 5 minutes prior to the end of the baking cycle. If your machine does not tell you how much time is left, try cutting the amount of sugar (which darkens the crust). If all of these methods fail, stop the machine at the end of the first kneading cycle and start the machine over again.

Brush butter or oil on the loaf while it is still hot to soften the crust. Milk will give a softer crust than water.

If the bread is not rising and/or is doughy, not baked enough and heavy —you should use the sweet or raisin cycle on your machine, if available. Natural sugars found in fruits, or too much butter or fat, may inhibit the rising of bread and cause the bread to bake improperly. Cut down on fruits and other sugary substances.

If the bread has large air bubbles— cut the amount of yeast used.

Some breads may be heavy and dense with the ingredients used. Non-wheat flours or meals, rye, oat, or corn with less gluten than wheat, will naturally be lower rising and denser than all wheat. In addition, ingredients such as wheat germ or bran actually break the gluten strands, causing breads to rise less. It may be helpful to add 1½ teaspoons to 2 tablespoons of vital (wheat) gluten to achieve a higher rise and/or a better texture when using large amounts of such grains. Other reasons for breads not rising include a large amount of salt, and/or not enough sugar or water. Sometimes raisins or similar ingredients do not mix into the dough evenly. Any dried fruit may be lightly floured to prevent pieces from sticking to each other. You may also add ingredients at the beginning of the second kneading cycle.

## GENERAL HINTS

• If breads don't rise consistently, try moving the machine to ensure that it is not in a draft.

• If that doesn't work, try using bottled water instead of tap water.

• If storing flour in the refrigerator, bring to room temperature or at least for 20 minutes before starting. Cold ingredients will cause the bread to not rise as well—it kills the yeast.

• If your machine does not have a preheat cycle, warm milk, water or other liquid in a microwave for about one minute, or until it feels warm to the inside of your wrist. Cut butter or margarine into quarters for even distribution. Butter and eggs may be used straight from the refrigerator or room temperature.

• When measuring honey, maple syrup, molasses, or similar sweeteners, measure the oil first. Use the oiled measuring spoon for the honey, etc. to slide off the spoon.

• Bananas should be very ripe and should be mashed or cut into small, 1-inch slices.

• Cheese should be lightly packed in the measuring cup.

• If making breads that rely on cheese, fruits or sour cream as a main source of liquid, do not use the timer and watch the dough carefully for moisture content. Add water or flour 1 tablespoon at a time after 5 minutes of kneading to ensure a proper texture. If desired, after dough has kneaded into a ball, stop the machine and restart it.

## OVERNIGHT DOUGH

Making breakfast breads on a timer is a very simple task. However, making dough in the evening for hot coffee rolls in the morning is also very simple and not as time consuming as you would think. Recommended recipes: Brioche, Almond Butter Crescents and variations, Cinnamon Rolls, and Sweet Rolls. Crusty Pizza Dough may also be made with a cold rise.

Place ingredients in machine and start the dough cycle in the normal manner. As soon as the machine has completed the first kneading and the dough is a nice, round, smooth ball, stop the machine. Depending on the pan itself or the space in the refrigerator, remove the pan, cover with plastic wrap, and refrigerate overnight. Otherwise, remove the dough, place in a greased bowl, and refrigerate overnight. The chilled dough will rise slowly through the night. Remove the dough in the morning, let sit for 5 to 10 minutes and then roll or shape according to directions. Let rise the second time in the normal fashion and bake according to recipe directions.

## DINNER BREAD BOWLS

Soup/Chili Bowls are a wonderful use of bread. Use your favorite dough to complement your hearty stew, bean soup, or chili. A 2 cup recipe makes 2 to 3 bowls, a 3 cup recipe makes 4 to 5 bowls and a 4 cup recipe makes 6 to 7 bowls.

Make the dough on the dough cycle. Upon completion of the cycle, remove dough and break into desired number of bread bowls. Shape each piece into large rolls or balls. Place on a lightly greased baking sheet, cover and let rise for 1 to 1½ hours. The "rolls" will be quite large. Bake in a preheated 350°F oven for 20 to 25 minutes or until golden brown. Place each "bowl" in a real bowl, cut off the top and scoop out the inside. Fill with stew or chili and serve with or without the top.

## BREAD WREATHS

A favorite Christmas gift is a bread wreath. Make dough on the dough cycle. Upon completion of the cycle, remove dough and divide into 10 to 15 balls. Roll each ball into a roll shape and place each roll on the outer rim of a lightly greased pizza pan so that they touch each other slightly. Cover and let rise for about 30 minutes. Bake in a preheated 350°F oven for 18 to 20 minutes.

## BAKING WITH KIDS

Baking with children is a great way to have special time and teach them too. Let the children help you measure the ingredients, learning basic math skills, and pour them into the pan bread—they'll gain a feeling of accomplishment. Also try some of the following:

• Put food coloring in the bread —"big, beautiful blue bread," red for Christmas or Valentines Day, etc. Green does not do well, but yellow, red and blue do.

• Let the children roll out pizza dough and let them make their own pizza.

• Let the children shape rolls. Sandwiches will taste better when they made the bread themselves.

## PIZZA PARTY

Depending on the group, each person or couple can bring ½ to 1 pound of cheese and a prepared, favorite pizza topping. Or provide all the ingredients and make several batches of dough. Give each person a choice of a sauce, cheese and toppings. As one person is making their pizza, another pizza is cooking.

To make multiple dough recipes: Add ingredients to the machine and start machine on dough cycle. As soon as the machine has finished the first kneading and the dough is a smooth, round ball, stop the machine and remove the dough from the pan. Place the dough in a lightly greased bowl, cover and let rise for 1 to 1½ hours. Repeat with a second batch of dough.

If desired, the covered bowl may be placed in the refrigerator and the dough allowed to cold-rise for 6 to 8 hours. Remove dough from refrigerator about 15 minutes before rolling out.

Use a preheated pizza stone in the oven, putting the pan on the stone until the pizza is firm enough to slide off onto the stone directly.

## LEFTOVER BREAD IDEAS

Some simple uses of leftover bread are croutons, bread crackers, garlic bread, bread stuffing, bread salad, egg strata for breakfast or dinner, cheese fondue or—of course—bread puddings.

# WHITE & CHEESE BREADS

# WHITE BREAD

This is a very rich bread—terrific for sandwiches. You'll find yourself going back for more and more. It is not, however, one of the more dietetic. Well worth the calories anyway! Use an egg white, egg yolk or 2 tablespoons egg substitute for ½ egg.

|  | SMALL | MEDIUM | LARGE |
|---|---|---|---|
| Water | ½ cup | ¾ cup | 1 cup |
| Margarine or butter | 2 Tbsp. | 2½ Tbsp. | 3 Tbsp. |
| Eggs | ½ | 1 | 1 |
| Sugar | 1½ Tbsp. | 2 Tbsp. | 2 Tbsp. |
| Salt | ¾ tsp. | 1 tsp. | 1½ tsp. |
| Bread flour | 2 cups | 3 cups | 3½ cups |
| Nonfat dry milk | 2½ Tbsp. | ¼ cup | ⅓ cup |
| Yeast | 1 tsp. | 1½ tsp. | 2 tsp. |
| Flour equivalent | 2 cups | 3 cups | 3½ cups |

**CYCLE:** basic cycle, no timer (eggs)
**SETTING:** medium

**VARIATION:** Add 1 to 2 teaspoons seeds such as caraway, anise, dill, fennel, flax, or sesame. It will be just enough to give a little extra flavor but not enough to overpower.

# ENGLISH MUFFIN BREAD

This is a really good, easy way to get that English muffin taste and texture. Great bread to set on the timer for a hot breakfast bread. In order to have the proper texture, there may be a sunken top to this bread.

| | SMALL | MEDIUM | LARGE |
|---|---|---|---|
| Water | ⅞ cup | 1¼ cups | 1½ cups |
| Sugar | 1½ tsp. | 2 tsp. | 1 Tbsp. |
| Salt | ¾ tsp. | 1 tsp. | 1 tsp. |
| Baking soda | ⅛ tsp. | ¼ tsp. | ½ tsp. |
| Bread flour | 2 cups | 3 cups | 3½ cups |
| Nonfat dry milk | 2 Tbsp. | 3 Tbsp. | ¼ cup |
| Yeast | 1 tsp. | 1½ tsp. | 2 tsp. |
| Flour equivalent | 2 cups | 3 cups | 3½ cups |

**CYCLE:** basic cycle, timer
**SETTING:** medium

# BUTTERMILK BREAD

You get great taste and texture and a light, fluffy bread without fresh buttermilk.

| | SMALL | MEDIUM | LARGE |
|---|---|---|---|
| Water | ⅔ cup | 1 cup | 1¼ cups |
| Margarine or butter | 1 Tbsp. | 2 Tbsp. | 2 Tbsp. |
| Sugar | 1 tsp. | 1½ tsp. | 2 tsp. |
| Salt | ½ tsp. | ¾ tsp. | 1 tsp. |
| Bread flour | 2 cups | 3 cups | 3½ cups |
| Buttermilk powder | 3 Tbsp. | ¼ cup | ⅓ cup |
| Yeast | 1½ tsp. | 2 tsp. | 2½ tsp. |
| Flour equivalent | 2 cups | 3 cups | 3½ cups |

**CYCLE:** basic cycle, timer
**SETTING:** medium

**AUSTRIAN MALT BREAD:** Use 2 tablespoons up to ¼ cup malted milk powder instead of the buttermilk powder. It can be found in the dry milk section of large grocery stores. The malt gives the bread an interesting flavor.

# PORTUGUESE SWEET BREAD

Maria and Manuel, from Portugal, contributed this recipe. She has experimented with recipes to closely resemble those of her country. This is one of my favorites.

| | SMALL | MEDIUM | LARGE |
|---|---|---|---|
| Milk | ½ cup | ¾ cup | ⅞ cup |
| Eggs | 1 | 1 | 2 |
| Margarine or butter | 1 Tbsp. | 1½ Tbsp. | 2 Tbsp. |
| Sugar | 3 Tbsp. | ¼ cup | ⅓ cup |
| Salt | ½ tsp. | ¾ tsp. | 1 tsp. |
| Bread flour | 2 cups | 2½ cups | 3 cups |
| Yeast | 1 tsp. | 1½ tsp. | 2 tsp. |
| Flour equivalent | 2 cups | 2½ cups | 3 cups |

**CYCLE:** sweet or basic cycle, no timer (eggs)
**SETTING:** light or medium

**VARIATIONS:** Add 1 to 2 teaspoons grated lemon zest or grated nutmeg with the dry ingredients.

# COTTAGE CHEESE BREAD

Warm the cottage cheese in the microwave for a minute or so. Watch the consistency and add water as necessary. Use an egg white or yolk or 2 tablespoons egg substitute for ½ egg.

|  | SMALL | MEDIUM | LARGE |
|---|---|---|---|
| Water | 3–4 Tbsp. | 3–4 Tbsp. | ¼–⅓ cup |
| Cottage cheese | ⅔ cup | ¾ cup | 1 cup |
| Margarine or butter | 1½ Tbsp. | 1½ Tbsp. | 2 Tbsp. |
| Eggs | ½ | 1 | 1 |
| Sugar | 2 tsp. | 1 Tbsp. | 1 Tbsp. |
| Baking soda | ⅛ tsp. | ¼ tsp. | ¼ tsp. |
| Salt | ¾ tsp. | 1 tsp. | 1 tsp. |
| Bread flour | 2 cups | 2½ cups | 3 cups |
| Yeast | 1½ tsp. | 2 tsp. | 2 tsp. |
| Flour equivalent | 2 cups | 3 cups | 3½ cups |

**CYCLE:** sweet or basic cycle, no timer (dairy products, watch consistency)
**SETTING:** medium

**DILL BREAD:** This is wonderful with either pasta or fish. Add 2 to 4 teaspoons dried dill weed to the above recipe.

# RICOTTA BREAD

This made a huge hit with friends and tasters who ranked it one of the best. It slices very well. Use an egg white, yolk or 2 tablespoons egg substitute for ½ egg. Warm the cheese for a high rise, but puncture the dough on the second rise if it rises too high.

| | SMALL | MEDIUM | LARGE |
|---|---|---|---|
| Milk | ¼ cup | ⅓ cup | ½ cup |
| Ricotta cheese | 1 cup | 1⅓ cups | 1½ cups |
| Margarine or butter | 2 Tbsp. | 2½ Tbsp. | 3 Tbsp. |
| Eggs | ½ | 1 | 1 |
| Sugar | 2½ Tbsp. | ¼ cup | ⅓ cup |
| Salt | 1 tsp. | 1 tsp. | 1½ tsp. |
| Bread flour | 2 cups | 3 cups | 3½ cups |
| Yeast | 1 tsp. | 1½ tsp. | 2 tsp. |
| Flour equivalent | 2 cups | 3 cups | 3½ cups |

**CYCLE:** sweet or basic cycle, no timer (dairy products, watch consistency)
**SETTING:** medium

**HERB RICOTTA BREAD:** Add 2 teaspoons up to 1½ tablespoons dried basil, oregano or parsley.

# ITALIAN BREAD

This is perfect bread with an Italian meal. Do not use the timer as you must watch the consistency of the dough and add water if necessary. To use this recipe for bread bowls with a hearty stew, see page 14.

| | SMALL | MEDIUM | LARGE |
|---|---|---|---|
| Water | ⅞ cup | 1¼ cups | 1½ cups |
| Sugar | 1 tsp. | 1½ tsp. | 2 tsp. |
| Salt | ¼ tsp. | ½ tsp. | ¾ tsp. |
| Bread flour | 2 cups | 3 cups | 3½ cups |
| Yeast | 1½ tsp. | 2 tsp. | 2½ tsp. |
| Flour equivalent | 2 cups | 3 cups | 3½ cups |

**CYCLE:** basic cycle, no timer (watch consistency)
**SETTING:** medium

# CHEDDAR CHEESE BREAD

This is a delicious bread. Use grated or shredded cheddar cheese and lightly pack it into the cup. The cheese may affect the consistency of the dough, so keep an eye on it and adjust the moisture as needed.

| | SMALL | MEDIUM | LARGE |
|---|---|---|---|
| Water or milk | ⅔ cup | 1 cup | 1¼ cups |
| Margarine or butter | 1 Tbsp. | 1 Tbsp. | 1½ Tbsp. |
| Cheddar cheese, shredded | ½ cup | ⅔ cup | ¾ cup |
| Sugar | 2 tsp. | 1 Tbsp. | 1½ Tbsp. |
| Salt | ½ tsp. | ¾ tsp. | 1 tsp. |
| Bread flour | 2 cups | 3 cups | 3½ cups |
| Yeast | 1 tsp. | 1½ tsp. | 2 tsp. |
| Flour equivalent | 2 cups | 3 cups | 3½ cups |

**CYCLE:** sweet or basic cycle, no timer (dairy products, watch consistency)
**SETTING:** medium

Because whole grains tend to be lower rising and denser, some recipes use higher amounts of flour than normal. If you have difficulty with whole wheat or whole grain loaves, allow the machine to knead one time and then turn off the machine and start it again, producing a longer kneading time. If you do not have a whole wheat cycle on your machine but do have a sweet cycle, try using the sweet cycle or the basic for whole grain breads.

# WHOLE WHEAT, GRAIN & CEREAL BREADS

# WHOLE WHEAT

This is my favorite whole wheat. It's a high-rising bread that slices very well.

| | SMALL | MEDIUM | LARGE |
|---|---|---|---|
| Water | ½ cup | ¾ cup | 1¼ cups |
| Margarine or butter | 2 Tbsp. | 3 Tbsp. | ¼ cup |
| Eggs | 1 | 1 | 1 |
| Sugar | 1½ Tbsp. | 2 Tbsp. | 2½ Tbsp. |
| Salt | ¾ tsp. | 1 tsp. | 1½ tsp. |
| Bread flour | 1½ cups | 2 cups | 2⅔ cups |
| Whole wheat flour | ¾ cup | 1 cup | 1⅓ cups |
| Yeast | 1 tsp. | 1½ tsp. | 2 tsp. |
| Flour equivalent | 2 cups | 3 cups | 4 cups |

**CYCLE:** whole wheat, sweet or basic cycle, timer
**SETTING:** medium

**VARIATION:** Add 1 to 2 teaspoons seeds such as caraway, anise, dill, fennel, flax or sesame. It will be just enough to give a little extra flavor but not enough to overpower.

# SPROUT BREAD

This is worth the trouble of sprouting the berries. The sprouts affect the amount of liquid required and you will have to adjust the consistency with water or flour.

| | SMALL | MEDIUM | LARGE |
|---|---|---|---|
| Water | ⅔ cup | ¾ cup | 1 cup |
| Margarine or butter | 1½ Tbsp. | 2 Tbsp. | 2½ Tbsp. |
| Sugar | 2 tsp. | 1 Tbsp. | 1½ Tbsp. |
| Salt | ½ tsp. | ¾ tsp. | 1 tsp. |
| Sprouted wheat berries | ⅓ cup | ½ cup | ⅔ cup |
| Bread flour | 2 cups | 2½ cups | 3 cups |
| Yeast | 1 tsp. | 1½ tsp. | 2½ tsp. |
| Flour equivalent | 2⅓ cups | 3 cups | 3⅔ cups |

**CYCLE:** whole wheat, sweet or basic cycle, no timer (check consistency)
**SETTING:** medium

Two to three days prior to making this bread, place ⅓ to ½ cup wheat berries in a sprouting jar (or any glass jar with cheesecloth tied down with a rubber band). Cover with water and allow to sit overnight (at least 12 hours). Drain and rinse again, right through the screen or cheesecloth, and set the jar mouth-side down at a 45° angle in a warm, dark place. Rinse sprouts twice a day. They are ready for use when you see small sprouts of about ⅛ to ¼ inch. (Wheat berry sprouts should be no longer than the berry itself.)

# NINE-GRAIN BREAD

Nine-grain cereal consists of cracked wheat, barley, corn, millet, oats, triticale, brown rice, soy, and flax seed and is available for purchase either in bulk or pre-boxed. It's available in a large grocery or a natural food store. Seven-grain cereal may also be used.

| | SMALL | MEDIUM | LARGE |
|---|---|---|---|
| Water | 1 cup | 1⅓ cups | 1½ cups |
| Margarine or butter | 2 Tbsp. | 2½ Tbsp. | 3 Tbsp. |
| Brown sugar | 1½ Tbsp. | 2 Tbsp. | 2½ Tbsp. |
| Salt | 1 tsp. | 1 tsp. | 1 tsp. |
| 9-grain cereal | 1 cup | 1⅓ cups | 1½ cups |
| Bread flour | 2 cups | 2⅔ cups | 3 cups |
| Yeast | 1 tsp. | 1½ tsp. | 2 tsp. |
| Flour equivalent | 3 cups | 4 cups | 4½ cups |

**CYCLE:** whole wheat, sweet or basic cycle, timer
**SETTING:** medium

# MULTI-GRAIN BREAD

This hearty, somewhat dense, full-of-fiber bread is wonderful with stew or soup. You can substitute cracked wheat for bulgur.

|  | SMALL | MEDIUM | LARGE |
|---|---|---|---|
| Water | 1⅛ cups | 1⅓ cups | 1½ cups |
| Vegetable oil | ½ Tbsp. | 2 Tbsp. | 2½ Tbsp. |
| Honey | 2 Tbsp. | 2½ Tbsp. | 3 Tbsp. |
| Salt | ¾ tsp. | 1 tsp. | 1½ tsp. |
| Bulgur wheat | ¼ cup | ⅓ cup | ½ cup |
| Wheat germ | 2 Tbsp. | 3 Tbsp. | ¼ cup |
| Wheat or oat bran | ½ cup | ⅔ cup | ¾ cup |
| Rye flour | ½ cup | ⅔ cup | ¾ cup |
| Rolled oats | ¼ cup | ⅓ cup | ½ cup |
| Bread flour | 1½ cups | 2¼ cups | 2½ cups |
| Vital gluten | 1½ Tbsp. | 2 Tbsp. | 2 Tbsp. |
| Yeast | 1½ tsp. | 2 tsp. | 2½ tsp. |
| Flour equivalent | 3 cups | 4 ½ cups | 5¼ cups |

**CYCLE:** whole wheat, sweet or basic cycle, no timer
**SETTING:** medium

# HIGH PROTEIN DIET (CORNELL) BREAD

This is a tasty dense loaf. The recipe is based on a formula for superior nutrition in bread by Cornell University. Wheat germ, soy flour and nonfat dry milk are added to each cup of flour in the Cornell Formula; this recipe makes it easier.

|  | SMALL | MEDIUM | LARGE |
|---|---|---|---|
| Water | 1 cup | 1¼ cups | 1½ cups |
| Vegetable oil | 1 Tbsp. | 1½ Tbsp. | 2 Tbsp. |
| Honey | 1 Tbsp. | 1½ Tbsp. | 2 Tbsp. |
| Salt | ¾ tsp. | 1 tsp. | 1 tsp. |
| Wheat germ | 2 Tbsp. | 3 Tbsp. | ¼ cup |
| Soy flour | ¼ cup | ⅓ cup | ½ cup |
| Whole wheat flour | 1 cup | 1⅓ cups | 1⅔ cups |
| Bread flour | 1½ cups | 1⅔ cups | 2 cups |
| Nonfat dry milk | ¼ cup | ⅓ cup | ½ cup |
| Vital gluten, optional | 1½ tsp. | 2 tsp. | 1 Tbsp. |
| Yeast | 1½ tsp. | 2 tsp. | 2½ tsp. |
| Flour equivalent | 3 cups | 4 cups | 5 cups |

**CYCLE:** whole wheat, sweet or basic cycle, timer
**SETTING:** medium

# WHOLE WHEAT OATMEAL BREAD

This great, wholesome bread slices well. It's one of my favorites. Use egg white, yolk or 2 tablespoons egg substitute for the ½ egg.

|  | SMALL | MEDIUM | LARGE |
|---|---|---|---|
| Water | ⅔ cup | 1 cup | 1⅓ cups |
| Margarine or butter | 2 Tbsp. | 2 Tbsp. | 3 Tbsp. |
| Eggs | ½ | 1 | 1 |
| Sugar | 1½ Tbsp. | 2 Tbsp. | 3 Tbsp. |
| Salt | ½ tsp. | ¾ tsp. | 1 tsp. |
| Rolled oats | ⅓ cup | ½ cup | ⅔ cup |
| Wheat germ | 3 Tbsp. | ¼ cup | ⅓ cup |
| Whole wheat flour | ½ cup | ¾ cup | 1 cup |
| Bread flour | 1½ cups | 2 cups | 3 cups |
| Yeast | 1½ tsp. | 2 tsp. | 2½ tsp. |
| Flour equivalent | 2½ cups | 3½ cups | 5 cups |

**CYCLE:** whole wheat, sweet or basic cycle, no timer (eggs)
**SETTING:** medium

# CRACKED WHEAT BREAD

One of the best. This natural, great-tasting and high-rising bread has a bit of crunchiness. If in doubt about the size to make, make the smallest size.

| | SMALL | MEDIUM | LARGE |
|---|---|---|---|
| Water | 1 cup | 1¼ cups | 1½ cups |
| Cracked wheat | ⅓ cup | ½ cup | ⅔ cup |
| Vegetable oil | 1½ Tbsp. | 2 Tbsp. | 2½ Tbsp. |
| Honey | 1 Tbsp. | 1 Tbsp. | 1½ Tbsp. |
| Salt | ½ tsp. | 1 tsp. | 1 tsp. |
| Whole wheat flour | ¾ cup | 1 cup | 1⅓ cups |
| Bread flour | 1 cup | 1½ cups | 2 cups |
| Vital gluten, optional | 1 Tbsp. | 2 Tbsp. | 2 Tbsp. |
| Yeast | 1 tsp. | 1½ tsp. | 2 tsp. |
| Flour equivalent | 2 cups | 3 cups | 4 cups |

**CYCLE:** whole wheat, sweet or basic cycle, timer
**SETTING:** medium

Soak the cracked wheat in the measured liquid for at least 1 hour. Add the water and cracked wheat with the liquid ingredients. Adjust the consistency with additional water or flour.

# OATMEAL BREAD

A terrific oatmeal loaf! Regular dry milk may be substituted for buttermilk powder.

|  | SMALL | MEDIUM | LARGE |
|---|---|---|---|
| Water | ¾ cup | ⅞ cup | 1⅓ cups |
| Margarine or butter | 2 Tbsp. | 2½ Tbsp. | 3 Tbsp. |
| Sugar | 1½ Tbsp. | 2 Tbsp. | 3 Tbsp. |
| Salt | ½ tsp. | ¾ tsp. | 1 tsp. |
| Rolled oats | ⅔ cup | 1 cup | 1⅓ cups |
| Bread flour | 1½ cups | 2 cups | 3 cups |
| Buttermilk powder | 3 Tbsp. | ¼ cup | ⅓ cup |
| Yeast | 1½ tsp. | 2 tsp. | 2½ tsp. |
| Flour equivalent | 2 cups | 3 cups | 4 cups |

**CYCLE:** whole wheat, sweet or basic cycle, timer
**SETTING:** medium

**CINNAMON OATMEAL BREAD:** Add 1 to 2 teaspoons cinnamon.
**RAISIN OATMEAL BREAD:** Add ¼ to ½ cup raisins with or without cinnamon (above).

# DARK PUMPERNICKEL

This heavy, dense bread is terrific with soup and or salad.

| | SMALL | MEDIUM | LARGE |
|---|---|---|---|
| Water | 1 cup | 1¼ cups | 1½ cups |
| Vegetable oil | 2 Tbsp. | 2½ Tbsp. | 3 Tbsp. |
| Molasses | 3 Tbsp. | ¼ cup | ⅓ cup |
| Unsweetened cocoa | 1½ Tbsp. | 2 Tbsp. | 2½ Tbsp. |
| Brown sugar | 1 Tbsp. | 1½ Tbsp. | 2 Tbsp. |
| Instant coffee granules | 1 tsp. | 1½ tsp. | 2 tsp. |
| Salt | ¾ tsp. | 1 tsp. | 1½ tsp. |
| Caraway seeds | 2 tsp. | 1 Tbsp. | 1 Tbsp. |
| Rye flour | ¾ cup | 1 cup | 1¼ cups |
| Whole wheat flour | ¾ cup | 1 cup | 1¼ cups |
| Bread flour | 1½ cups | 2 cups | 2½ cups |
| Yeast | 1½ tsp. | 2 tsp. | 2½ tsp. |
| Flour equivalent | 3 cups | 4 cups | 5 cups |

**CYCLE:** whole wheat, sweet or basic cycle, timer
**SETTING:** medium

# HONEY CORNMEAL BREAD

This is a very tasty, slightly sweet cornmeal loaf. The dough may appear wet, but it should be high-rising and light in texture as a result.

|  | SMALL | MEDIUM | LARGE |
|---|---|---|---|
| Water | ½ cup | ¾ cup | 1 cup |
| Vegetable oil | 1 Tbsp. | 1½ Tbsp. | 2 Tbsp. |
| Honey | 2 Tbsp. | 3 Tbsp. | ¼ cup |
| Eggs | 2 | 3 | 4 |
| Salt | ½ tsp. | 1 tsp. | 1 tsp. |
| Cornmeal | ⅔ cup | 1 cup | 1⅓ cups |
| Whole wheat flour | ⅓ cup | ½ cup | ⅔ cup |
| Bread flour | 1 cup | 1½ cups | 2 cups |
| Yeast | 1 tsp. | 1½ tsp. | 2½ tsp. |
| Flour equivalent | 2 cups | 3 cups | 4 cups |

**CYCLE:** whole wheat, sweet or basic cycle, no timer (eggs)
**SETTING:** medium

# QUINOA BREAD

The quinoa gives this bread a nutty flavor. Great source of protein and calcium—worth trying. Quinoa flour is available at large grocery and health food stores.

|  | SMALL | MEDIUM | LARGE |
|---|---|---|---|
| Water | ¾ cup | 1⅛ cups | 1¼ cups |
| Margarine or butter | 2 Tbsp. | ¼ cup | ¼ cup |
| Sugar | 1½ tsp. | 2 tsp. | 1 Tbsp. |
| Salt | ½ tsp. | 1 tsp. | 1½ tsp. |
| Quinoa flour | ⅓ cup | ½ cup | ¾ cup |
| Bread flour | 2 cups | 2½ cups | 3 cups |
| Yeast | 1 tsp. | 1½ tsp. | 2 tsp. |
| Flour equivalent | 2⅓ cups | 3 cups | 3¾ cups |

**CYCLE:** whole wheat, sweet or basic, timer
**SETTING:** medium

# NEW YORK RYE BREAD

This is a low-rising, dense, flavorful loaf. If you want a lighter loaf, add vital wheat gluten, available at health food stores. Caraway may be adjusted to taste. Serve this bread, dried, as bread crackers, with cheddar cheese and caraway seeds.

| | SMALL | MEDIUM | LARGE |
|---|---|---|---|
| Water | ⅞ cup | 1⅛ cups | 1⅓ cups |
| Vegetable oil | 1 Tbsp. | 1⅓ Tbsp. | 1½ Tbsp. |
| Honey | 1½ Tbsp. | 2 Tbsp. | 2½ Tbsp. |
| Salt | ¾ tsp. | 1 tsp. | 1 tsp. |
| Caraway seeds | 2 tsp. | 1 Tbsp. | 1 Tbsp. |
| Rye flour | 1 cup | 1⅓ cups | 1½ cups |
| Bread flour | 1¾ cups | 2¼ cups | 2⅔ cups |
| Vital gluten, optional | 2 tsp. | 1 Tbsp. | 1½ Tbsp. |
| Nonfat dry milk | 3 Tbsp. | ¼ cup | ⅓ cup |
| Yeast | 1½ tsp. | 2 tsp. | 2½ tsp. |
| Flour equivalent | 2¾ cups | 3½+ cups | 4½+ cups |

**CYCLE:** whole wheat, sweet or basic cycle, timer
**SETTING:** medium

# THREE-SEED BREAD

This bread has a wonderful taste and texture. Feel free to experiment with different seeds. Try combinations of anise, fennel, caraway or any other seeds. This bread is great toasted or broiled with cheese.

| | SMALL | MEDIUM | LARGE |
|---|---|---|---|
| Water | 1 cup | 1½ cups | 1¾ cups |
| Vegetable oil | 1½ Tbsp. | 2 Tbsp. | 3 Tbsp. |
| Honey | 1½ tsp. | 2 tsp. | 1 Tbsp. |
| Salt | ½ tsp. | ¾ tsp. | 1 tsp. |
| Sunflower seeds | 3 Tbsp. | ¼ cup | ⅓ cup |
| Sesame seeds | 1½ Tbsp. | 2 Tbsp. | 3 Tbsp. |
| Poppy seeds | 1 Tbsp. | 1½ Tbsp. | 2 Tbsp. |
| Whole wheat flour | 1 cup | 1⅓ cups | 1½ cups |
| Bread flour | 2 cups | 2¾ cups | 3 cups |
| Nonfat milk powder | 3 Tbsp. | ¼ cup | ¼ cup |
| Yeast | 1 tsp. | 2 tsp. | 2½ tsp. |
| Flour equivalent | 3 cups | 4+ cups | 4½ cups |

**CYCLE:** whole wheat, sweet or basic cycle, timer
**SETTING:** medium

# AMARANTH NUT BREAD

A wonderful nutty bread. It may be used for sandwiches, or as a dessert bread. Use an egg white, yolk or 2 tablespoons egg substitute for ½ egg.

| | SMALL | MEDIUM | LARGE |
|---|---|---|---|
| Water | ⅔ cup | 1 cup | 1¼ cups |
| Vegetable oil | 1 Tbsp. | 2 Tbsp. | 2½ Tbsp. |
| Honey | 2 Tbsp. | 3 Tbsp. | ¼ cup |
| Eggs | ½ | 1 | 1 |
| Vanilla extract | ½ tsp. | 1 tsp. | 1 tsp. |
| Salt | ½ tsp. | 1 tsp. | 1½ tsp. |
| Amaranth flour | ⅓ cup | ½ cup | ⅔ cup |
| Bread flour | 1¾ cups | 2½ cups | 3⅓ cups |
| Nonfat milk powder | 2 Tbsp. | 3 Tbsp. | ¼ cup |
| Yeast | 1 tsp. | 1½ tsp. | 2 tsp. |

*After the first kneading, add:*

| | | | |
|---|---|---|---|
| Chopped walnuts | ⅓ cup | ½ cup | ⅔ cup |
| Flour equivalent | 2½ cups | 3½ cups | 4⅔ cups |

**CYCLE:** whole wheat, sweet or basic cycle, no timer (eggs)
**SETTING:** medium

# SOURDOUGH BREADS

# SOURDOUGH STARTER

A true sourdough starter is flour and milk or water that sits at room temperature for several days and catches live yeast from the air. Most starter recipes today include yeast as an original starter ingredient as it is much easier and less time-consuming. In addition, many sourdough bread recipes also add yeast as it provides a higher rising, lighter loaf.

A sourdough starter should be kept in a glass or plastic bowl with a tight-fitting lid. **To make your starter, mix together: 2 cups lukewarm milk, 2 cups bread flour and 2½ teaspoons (1 package) yeast.**

Mix the starter with an electric hand-held mixer on the lowest setting. Cover the starter and place in a warm, draft-free location for 4 to 7 days, gently stirring it once a day. You may notice that the mixture bubbles and may overflow the bowl. This is an indication of a healthy fermenting process. A sour-smelling liquid may form on top of the starter, which should simply be stirred back in.

If the starter ever changes colors, to purple, for example, discard and start another one. After allowing the starter to sit for 4 to 7 days, it is ready to be used. Take out whatever portion your recipe calls for and put it into the machine as you would any liquid ingredient.

After removing a portion from the starter, the remaining starter must be "fed." Simply add equal portions of milk or water and flour as was used. If 1 cup of starter was used, replace it with 1 cup of water and 1 cup of bread flour.

Some hints on feeding your starter: Always use the same kind of flour. If you used bread flour in your original starter, use bread flour to feed it. Also, alternate between milk and water for each feeding. If the original liquid ingredient was milk, the first liquid feeding should be with water. After feeding your starter, let it sit at room temperature for approximately 1 day and then refrigerate.

You must use a portion of the starter at least once a week. If you choose not to bake sourdough breads that often, then remove a cup of your starter and feed it as though you used some during the week. If this is not done, your starter will turn rancid and have to be replaced. Should you be away on vacation or otherwise unable to tend to the starter, freeze it. Upon your return, thaw it in the refrigerator and then remove a portion and feed it as soon as you are able.

Another hint is to put the ingredients on the timer cycle for early morning baking. The milk put in the night before adds a little more sour taste. If the bread is getting too sour for you, feed with water more often than milk.

Always check the consistency of the dough. The starter itself may vary from one day to the next and it is not uncommon to have to adjust the dough with water or flour.

If you use your starter frequently and/or it is very active and strong, it may be necessary to decrease the amount of yeast given in the recipe. This will require experimentation. It may even be possible to omit the yeast altogether if the bread is rising sufficiently with just the sourdough starter.

Many of the recipes in this chapter were adapted from ethnic recipes, calling for a high amount of salt. If you feel the bread is too salty, you may safely cut the amount of salt to approximately 1 teaspoon for a large size recipe.

# SOURDOUGH BREAD

This compares favorably to the famous San Francisco sourdoughs. Adjust the consistency with the milk while the dough is kneading.

| | SMALL | MEDIUM | LARGE |
|---|---|---|---|
| Starter | ¾ cup | 1 cup | 1⅓ cups |
| Margarine or butter | 1 Tbsp. | 2 Tbsp. | 2 Tbsp. |
| Sugar | 1½ Tbsp. | 2 Tbsp. | 2½ Tbsp. |
| Salt | 1 tsp. | 1½ tsp. | 1½ tsp. |
| Bread flour | 2 cups | 3 cups | 3½ cups |
| Yeast | 1 tsp. | 1½ tsp. | 2 tsp. |
| Milk | 3 Tbsp.–⅓ cup | ¼–⅔ cup | ¼–¾ cup |
| Flour equivalent | 2⅓ cups | 3½ cups | 4¼ cups |

**CYCLE:** basic, no timer (watch consistency)
**SETTING:** medium

# SOURDOUGH WHEAT BREAD

A delicious sourdough with the benefits of whole wheat flour.
Adjust the consistency with the milk while the dough is kneading.

| | SMALL | MEDIUM | LARGE |
|---|---|---|---|
| Starter | ⅞ cup | 1 cup | 1½ cups |
| Margarine or butter | 1 Tbsp. | 2 Tbsp. | 2½ Tbsp. |
| Sugar | 1½ Tbsp. | 2 Tbsp. | 2½ Tbsp. |
| Salt | 1 tsp. | 1½ tsp. | 1½ tsp. |
| Whole wheat flour | ¾ cup | 1 cup | 1½ cups |
| Bread flour | 1½ cups | 2 cups | 2½ cups |
| Yeast | 1 tsp. | 2 tsp. | 2 tsp. |
| Milk | 3 Tbsp.–⅓ cup | ¼ – ⅔ cup | ¼ – ¾ cup |
| Flour equivalent | 2⅓ cups | 3½ cups | 4¾ cups |

**CYCLE:** basic, no timer (watch consistency)
**SETTING:** medium

## RYE STARTER

|  | SMALL | MEDIUM | LARGE |
|---|---|---|---|
| Yeast | 1 tsp. | 1 tsp. | 1½ tsp. |
| Warm milk (115°F) | ½ cup | ¾ cup | 1 cup |
| Rye flour | ½ cup | ¾ cup | 1 cup |

To prepare: Sprinkle yeast over warm milk and stir until dissolved; stir in rye flour. Cover and let stand at room temperature for 3 days, stirring once a day. Use the entire starter in your bread recipe.

## SOURDOUGH RYE BREAD

This slightly sour loaf is very light and has its own starter, which is used in its entirety in the recipe. Molasses may be substituted for barley malt syrup.

|  | SMALL | MEDIUM | LARGE |
|---|---|---|---|
| Rye Starter | * | * | * |
| Water | ⅓ cup | ½ cup | ⅔ cup |
| Eggs | ½ | 1 | 1 |
| Vegetable oil | 1 Tbsp. | 1½ Tbsp. | 2 Tbsp. |
| Barley malt syrup | 1 Tbsp. | 1½ Tbsp. | 2 Tbsp. |
| Salt | 1 tsp. | 1½ tsp. | 2 tsp. |
| Caraway seeds | 2 tsp. | 1 Tbsp. | 1⅓ Tbsp. |
| Bread flour | 1¾ cups | 2½ cups | 3 cups |
| Rye flour | ½ cup | ¾ cup | 1 cup |
| Yeast | 1 tsp. | 1½ tsp. | 2½ tsp. |
| Flour equivalent | 2¾ cups | 4 cups | 5 cups |

**CYCLE:** basic cycle, no timer (watch consistency)
**SETTING:** medium

# SOURDOUGH FRENCH BREAD

This is absolutely delicious —great for sandwiches. Adjust the consistency with the water while the dough is kneading.

| | SMALL | MEDIUM | LARGE |
|---|---|---|---|
| Starter | ⅔ cup | 1 cup | 1⅓ cups |
| Sugar | 1 tsp. | 1½ tsp. | 2 tsp. |
| Salt | ½ tsp. | ¾ tsp. | 1 tsp. |
| Bread flour | 2 cups | 3 cups | 4 cups |
| Yeast | 1 tsp. | 1½ tsp. | 2 tsp. |
| Water | ¼–⅓ cup | ½–⅔ cup | ⅔–¾ cup |
| Flour equivalent | 2⅓ cups | 3½ cups | 4⅔ cups |

**CYCLE:** basic, no timer (watch consistency)
**SETTING:** medium

# SOURDOUGH CORNMEAL BREAD

This is a unique, delicious bread. Adjust the consistency with the milk while the dough is kneading.

| | SMALL | MEDIUM | LARGE |
|---|---|---|---|
| Starter | ⅔ cup | 1 cup | 1⅓ cups |
| Margarine or butter | 1 Tbsp. | 1½ Tbsp. | 2 Tbsp. |
| Sugar | 1 Tbsp. | 1½ Tbsp. | 2 Tbsp. |
| Salt | ½ tsp. | ¾ tsp. | 1 tsp. |
| Cornmeal | ⅔ cup | 1 cup | 1⅓ cups |
| Bread flour | 1½ cups | 2½ cups | 2⅔ cups |
| Yeast | 1 tsp. | 1½ tsp. | 2 tsp. |
| Milk | 2–4 Tbsp. | ¼–⅓ cup | ⅓–½ cup |
| Flour equivalent | 3 cups | 4 cups | 4⅔ cups |

**CYCLE:** basic, no timer (watch consistency)
**SETTING:** medium

# SOURDOUGH OATMEAL BREAD

This is a very moist sourdough bread. Adjust the consistency with the milk while the dough is kneading.

|  | SMALL | MEDIUM | LARGE |
| --- | --- | --- | --- |
| Starter | ¾ cup | 1 cup | 1¼ cups |
| Margarine or butter | 1 Tbsp. | 1½ Tbsp. | 2 Tbsp. |
| Sugar | 1 Tbsp. | 1½ Tbsp. | 2 Tbsp. |
| Salt | ¾ tsp. | 1 tsp. | 1 tsp. |
| Rolled oats | ¾ cup | 1 cup | 1¼ cups |
| Bread flour | 2¼ cups | 3 cups | 3½ cups |
| Yeast | 1½ tsp. | 2 tsp. | 2 tsp. |
| Milk | ⅓–½ cup | ½–⅔ cup | ⅔–¾ cup |
| Flour equivalent | 3½ cups | 4½ cups | 5½ cups |

**CYCLE:** basic, no timer (watch consistency)
**SETTING:** medium

# SPECIALTY BREADS

# APPLE CHUNK BREAD

The apples add moisture to the dough. Add apples at the beginning of the second kneading cycle. Add 1 to 2 tablespoon flour to adjust consistency if necessary. Serve with an optional icing.

|  | SMALL | MEDIUM | LARGE |
|---|---|---|---|
| Milk | ⅔ cup | 1 cup | 1¼ cups |
| Vegetable oil | 2 Tbsp. | 3 Tbsp. | 3 Tbsp. |
| Sugar | 1½ Tbsp. | 2 Tbsp. | 2½ Tbsp. |
| Cinnamon | ½ tsp. | ½ tsp. | 1 tsp. |
| Salt | 1 tsp. | 1½ tsp. | 1½ tsp. |
| Bread flour | 2 cups | 3 cups | 3½ cups |
| Yeast | 1 tsp. | 1½ tsp. | 2 tsp. |

*After the first kneading, add:*

|  | SMALL | MEDIUM | LARGE |
|---|---|---|---|
| Apple, medium, peeled, diced | ½ | 1½ | 1½ |
| Chopped walnuts | ⅓ cup | ½ cup | ⅔ cup |
| Flour equivalent | 2 cups | 3 cups | 4 cups |

**CYCLE:** sweet or basic cycle, no timer (watch consistency)
**SETTING:** light to medium
**VARIATION:** Stir 2 cups confectioners' sugar together with 1 to 2 tablespoons water until smooth. Brush on loaf and sprinkle with ¼ to ½ chopped walnuts.

# BANANA OATMEAL BREAD

This low-rising bread has a slight taste of banana with the "feel" of oatmeal. The flavor of the banana seems to be stronger when the bread is toasted. Use fully ripe bananas and adjust the dough consistency with the extra water if you need to.

| | SMALL | MEDIUM | LARGE |
|---|---|---|---|
| Water | ⅓–½ cup | ½–⅔ cup | ½–¾ cup |
| Mashed banana | ¾ cup | 1 cup | 1¼ cups |
| Vegetable oil | 2 Tbsp. | 2½ Tbsp. | 3 Tbsp. |
| Sugar | 1 Tbsp. | 1½ Tbsp. | 2 Tbsp. |
| Salt | 1 tsp. | 1 tsp. | 1½ tsp. |
| Rolled oats | 1 cup | 1⅓ cups | 1¾ cups |
| Bread flour | 2 cups | 2⅔ cups | 3 cups |
| Yeast | 1½ tsp. | 2 tsp. | 2½ tsp. |
| Flour equivalent | 3 cups | 4 cups | 4¾ cups |

**CYCLE:** sweet, basic, no timer (watch consistency)
**SETTING:** light to medium

# IRISH SODA BREAD

While at first you may wonder about the caraway seed and raisin combination, once you've tried it, you'll be hooked.

|  | SMALL | MEDIUM | LARGE |
|---|---|---|---|
| Buttermilk | ¾ cup | 1⅛ cups | 1⅓ cups |
| Margarine or butter | 1½ Tbsp. | 2 Tbsp. | 3 Tbsp. |
| Sugar | 1½ Tbsp. | 2 Tbsp. | 2½ Tbsp. |
| Salt | ¾ tsp. | 1 tsp. | 1 tsp. |
| Baking soda | ¼ tsp. | ½ tsp. | ½ tsp. |
| Caraway seeds | 1½ tsp. | 2 tsp. | 1 Tbsp. |
| Bread flour | 2 cups | 3 cups | 3½ cups |
| Yeast | 1½ tsp. | 2 tsp. | 2½ tsp. |

*After the first kneading, add:*

| Raisins | ¼ cup | ⅓ cup | ½ cup |
|---|---|---|---|
| Flour equivalent | 2 cups | 3 cups | 3½ cups |

**CYCLE:** sweet, basic, no timer (add raisins at beep)
**SETTING:** light to medium

# POTATO BREAD

This potato bread is really good alone or as sandwich bread. The potatoes give it just a little extra flavor. This is high-rising. If in doubt about the size, use a smaller size. This bread slices very well. Use an egg yolk, white or 2 tablespoons egg substitute for the ½ egg. A few hours before making the bread, boil 1 to 2 peeled potatoes. Save water to use in bread. Mash potatoes, without milk or butter, and let cool to lukewarm or room temperature.

| | SMALL | MEDIUM | LARGE |
|---|---|---|---|
| Potato water | ½ cup | ⅔ cup | ¾ cup |
| Margarine or butter | 2 Tbsp. | 2½ Tbsp. | 3 Tbsp. |
| Eggs | ½ | ½ | 1 |
| Mashed potato | ⅓ cup | ⅓ cup | ½ cup |
| Sugar | 1½ Tbsp. | 2 Tbsp. | 2 Tbsp. |
| Salt | ¾ tsp. | 1 tsp. | 1 tsp. |
| Bread flour | 2 cups | 2½ cups | 3 cups |
| Nonfat dry milk | 2 Tbsp. | ¼ cup | ⅓ cup |
| Yeast | 1 tsp. | 1½ tsp. | 2 tsp. |
| Flour equivalent | 2 cups | 2½ cups | 3 cups |

**CYCLE:** sweet, basic, no timer (watch consistency)
**SETTING:** light to medium

# LEMON BREAD

This lightly colored bread has a subtle, pleasing flavor. The lemon zest may be adjusted to taste. Serve as a side to a fish or chicken dinner.

|  | SMALL | MEDIUM | LARGE |
|---|---|---|---|
| Water | ⅔ cup | 1 cup | 1¼ cups |
| Margarine or butter | 1 Tbsp. | 2 Tbsp. | 2 Tbsp. |
| Grated lemon zest | ¾ tsp. | 1 tsp. | 1½ tsp |
| Sugar | ½ tsp. | ¾ tsp. | 1 tsp. |
| Salt | ¼ tsp. | ½ tsp. | ¾ tsp. |
| Bread flour | 2 cups | 3 cups | 3½ cups |
| Nonfat dry milk | 2 Tbsp. | ¼ cup | ⅓ cup |
| Yeast | 1 tsp. | 1½ tsp. | 2 tsp. |
| Flour equivalent | 3 cups | 4 cups | 4¾ cups |

**CYCLE:** sweet, basic, timer
**SETTING:** medium

# ORANGE CINNAMON BREAD

This makes wonderful French toast or regular toast with butter and preserves. Both the cinnamon and the orange zest may be adjusted to taste.

|  | SMALL | MEDIUM | LARGE |
|---|---|---|---|
| Orange juice | ¾ cup | 1⅛ cups | 1⅓ cups |
| Margarine or butter | 1 Tbsp. | 2 Tbsp. | 2 Tbsp. |
| Cinnamon | 1 tsp. | 2 tsp. | 1 Tbsp. |
| Grated orange zest | ¾ tsp. | 1 tsp. | 1 tsp |
| Salt | ½ tsp. | ¾ tsp. | 1 tsp. |
| Sugar | 1 tsp. | 2 tsp. | 1 Tbsp. |
| Bread flour | 2 cups | 3 cups | 3½ cups |
| Yeast | 1½ tsp. | 2 tsp. | 2½ tsp. |
| Flour equivalent | 2 cups | 3 cups | 3½ cups |

**CYCLE:** sweet, basic, no timer (watch consistency)
**SETTING:** light to medium

**ORANGE CRAISIN BREAD:** Add ¼, ½ or ¾ cup Craisins, after the first kneading.

# RAISIN BREAD

Any of the variations make fabulous French toast.

|  | SMALL | MEDIUM | LARGE |
|---|---|---|---|
| Water | ¾ cup | 1⅛ cups | 1¼ cups |
| Margarine or butter | 2 Tbsp. | 2½ Tbsp. | 3 Tbsp. |
| Sugar | 1½ Tbsp. | 2 Tbsp. | 2 Tbsp. |
| Salt | ¾ tsp. | 1 tsp. | 1 tsp. |
| Bread flour | 2 cups | 3 cups | 3½ cups |
| Yeast | 1 tsp. | 1½ tsp. | 2 tsp. |

*After the first kneading, add:*

|  | SMALL | MEDIUM | LARGE |
|---|---|---|---|
| Raisins | ½ cup | ¾ cup | 1 cup |
| Flour equivalent | 2 cups | 3 cups | 3½ cups |

**CYCLE:** sweet, basic, no timer (adding raisins)
**SETTING:** light to medium

**VARIATIONS:** All the following ingredients are put in the machine when it beeps or after the first kneading.

**CINNAMON RAISIN:** Add raisins and 2 to 3 teaspoons cinnamon
**APRICOT:** Add ½ to 1 cup chopped dried apricots
**DRIED FRUIT:** Add ½ to 1 cup chopped mixed dried fruit
**ORANGE RAISIN:** Add raisins and ⅓ to 1 teaspoon grated orange zest

# PUMPKIN/WINTER SQUASH BREAD

This bread is great way to hide vegetables from finicky eaters. Use cooked, mashed acorn, butternut, or hubbard squash or canned pumpkin in this recipe. Watch the consistency.

|  | SMALL | MEDIUM | LARGE |
|---|---|---|---|
| Water | ½ cup | ¾ cup | 1 cup |
| Winter squash, cooked, mashed | ⅓ cup | ⅔ cup | ¾ cup |
| Vegetable oil | 1½ Tbsp. | 2 Tbsp. | 3 Tbsp. |
| Honey | 1½ Tbsp. | 2 Tbsp. | 3 Tbsp. |
| Salt | 1 tsp. | 1½ tsp. | 2 tsp. |
| Cinnamon | ¾ tsp. | 1 tsp. | 1⅓ tsp. |
| Ground allspice | ¼ tsp. | ½ tsp. | ¾ tsp. |
| Nutmeg | ⅛ tsp. | ¼ tsp. | ½ tsp. |
| Ground cloves | ⅛ tsp. | ¼ tsp. | ½ tsp. |
| Whole wheat flour | ⅓ cup | ½ cup | ⅔ cup |
| Bread flour | 1⅔ cups | 2½ cups | 3⅓ cups |
| Yeast | 1 tsp. | 1½ tsp. | 2½ tsp. |
| Flour equivalent | 2 cups | 3 cups | 4 cups |

**CYCLE:** sweet, basic, no timer (watch consistency)
**SETTING:** light to medium

# ZUCCHINI WHEAT BREAD

Zucchini lovers will be especially happy with this one. Toasting brings out a stronger flavor. Watch the consistency and adjust with water or flour as needed.

| | SMALL | MEDIUM | LARGE |
|---|---|---|---|
| Shredded zucchini | ½ cup | ¾ cup | 1 cup |
| Water | ½ cup | ¾ cup | 1 cup |
| Vegetable oil | 2 Tbsp. | 3 Tbsp. | ¼ cup |
| Honey | 2 Tbsp. | 3 Tbsp. | 3 Tbsp. |
| Salt | ½ tsp. | ¾ tsp. | 1 tsp. |
| Grated orange zest | ¾ tsp. | 1 tsp | 1½ tsp. |
| Wheat germ | 3 Tbsp. | ¼ cup | ⅓ cup |
| Whole wheat flour | 1 cup | 1½ cups | 2 cups |
| Bread flour | 1 cup | 1½ cups | 2 cups |
| Yeast | 1 tsp. | 1½ tsp. | 2 tsp. |
| Flour equivalent | 2 cups | 3 cups | 4 cups |

**CYCLE:** sweet, basic, no timer (watch consistency)
**SETTING:** light to medium

# CARROT BREAD

This delicious, healthy bread is a good way to get your beta carotene! Much of the liquid comes from the grated carrot —watch the consistency and add water or flour if necessary. There is a high amount of low-rising flour, see page 13.

| | SMALL | MEDIUM | LARGE |
|---|---|---|---|
| Water | ¾ cup | ⅞ cup | 1¼ cups |
| Vegetable oil | 1 Tbsp. | 1½ Tbsp. | 2 Tbsp. |
| Carrot, grated | ½ cup | ⅔ cup | ¾ cup |
| Brown sugar | 1½ Tbsp. | 2 Tbsp. | 2½ Tbsp. |
| Salt | 1 tsp. | 1 tsp. | 1½ tsp. |
| Rolled oats | 1 cup | 1⅓ cups | 1½ cups |
| Whole wheat flour | ½ cup | ⅔ cup | ¾ cup |
| Bread flour | 1½ cups | 2 cups | 2½ cups |
| Nonfat dry milk | 3 Tbsp. | ¼ cup | ⅓ cup |
| Yeast | 1 tsp. | 1½ tsp. | 2 tsp. |
| Flour equivalent | 3 cups | 4 cups | 4¾ cups |

**CYCLE:** sweet, basic, no timer (watch consistency)
**SETTING:** light to medium

# CHRISTMAS ANISE BREAD

Anise adds nice flavor to this bread but is not overwhelming. If you want a stronger tasting bread, you may safely double the amount of anise and other spices. This makes delicious French toast.

|  | SMALL | MEDIUM | LARGE |
|---|---|---|---|
| Milk | ⅔ cup | 1 cup | 1¼ cups |
| Margarine or butter | 2 Tbsp. | 2½ Tbsp. | 3 Tbsp. |
| Sugar | 1 Tbsp. | 1½ Tbsp. | 2 Tbsp. |
| Salt | ½ tsp. | ¾ tsp. | 1 tsp. |
| Anise seeds | 1 tsp. | 1½ tsp. | 2 tsp. |
| Mace | pinch | ⅛ tsp. | ¼ tsp. |
| Nutmeg | pinch | ⅛ tsp. | ¼ tsp. |
| Grated lemon zest | ½ tsp | ¾ tsp. | 1 tsp. |
| Grated orange zest | ½ tsp | ¾ tsp. | 1 tsp. |
| Bread flour | 2 cups | 3 cups | 3½ cups |
| Yeast | 1½ tsp. | 2 tsp. | 2½ tsp. |
| Flour equivalent | 2 cups | 3 cups | 3½ cups |

**CYCLE:** sweet, basic, timer
**SETTING:** medium

# PANETTONE

Candied fruit is traditionally used in panettone recipes, but some machines have difficulty baking the high sugar content. Try dried mixed fruits instead. Glass-domed machines should make the medium size. This is perfect for French toast.

|                        | SMALL      | MEDIUM    | LARGE      |
|------------------------|-----------|-----------|-----------|
| Water                  | ½ cup     | ⅔ cup     | ¾ cup     |
| Margarine or butter    | 3 Tbsp.   | 4 Tbsp.   | 5 Tbsp.   |
| Eggs                   | 1         | 1½        | 1½        |
| Sugar                  | 3 Tbsp.   | ¼ cup     | ⅓ cup     |
| Salt                   | ½ tsp.    | ¾ tsp.    | 1 tsp.    |
| Grated lemon zest      | 1 tsp     | 1½ tsp.   | 1½ tsp.   |
| Bread flour            | 2 cups    | 3 cups    | 3½ cups   |
| Yeast                  | 1 tsp.    | 1½ tsp.   | 2 tsp.    |

*After the first kneading, add:*

|                          | SMALL     | MEDIUM    | LARGE     |
|--------------------------|-----------|-----------|-----------|
| Mixed dried fruit, chopped | 2 Tbsp.  | 3 Tbsp.   | ¼ cup     |
| Chopped nuts             | 2 Tbsp.   | 3 Tbsp.   | ¼ cup     |
| Flour equivalent         | 2 cups    | 3 cups    | 3½ cups   |

**CYCLE:** sweet, basic, no timer (add fruit/nuts at beep)
**SETTING:** light to medium

# COFFEE SPICE BREAD

This is similar in taste to a brown bread and a great way to use up that leftover coffee regular or decaf!

| | SMALL | MEDIUM | LARGE |
|---|---|---|---|
| Brewed coffee | ½ cup | ¾ cup | 1 cup |
| Vegetable oil | 2 Tbsp. | 2½ Tbsp. | 3 Tbsp. |
| Eggs | 1 | 1 | 1 |
| Sugar | 2 Tbsp. | 3 Tbsp. | ¼ cup |
| Salt | ¾ tsp. | 1 tsp. | 1 tsp. |
| Cinnamon | ¾ tsp. | 1 tsp. | 1 tsp. |
| Ground cloves | ⅛ tsp. | ¼ tsp. | ½ tsp. |
| Ground allspice | ⅛ tsp. | ¼ tsp. | ½ tsp. |
| Bread flour | 2 cups | 3 cups | 3½ cups |
| Yeast | 1 tsp. | 1½ tsp. | 2 tsp. |
| Flour equivalent | 2 cups | 3 cups | 3½ cups |

**CYCLE:** basic, timer
**SETTING:** medium

# STOLLEN

If this bread does not bake properly, reduce the amount of fruits.

|  | SMALL | MEDIUM | LARGE |
|---|---|---|---|
| Milk | ½ – ⅔ cup | ⅔ – ¾ cup | ⅞ – 1 cup |
| Margarine or butter | 2 Tbsp. | 3 Tbsp. | ¼ cup |
| Eggs | 1 | 1 | 1 |
| Almond extract | ¼ tsp. | ¼ tsp. | ½ tsp. |
| Rum extract | ¼ tsp. | ¼ tsp. | ½ tsp. |
| Sugar | 2 Tbsp. | 3 Tbsp. | ¼ cup |
| Salt | ¾ tsp. | 1 tsp. | 1 tsp. |
| Mace | ⅛ tsp. | ⅛ tsp. | ¼ tsp. |
| Cardamom | pinch | pinch | ⅛ tsp. |
| Grated lemon zest | 1½ tsp | 2 tsp. | 1 Tbsp. |
| Grated orange zest | 1½ tsp | 2 tsp. | 1 Tbsp. |
| Bread flour | 2 cups | 3 cups | 3½ cups |
| Yeast | 1 tsp. | 1½ tsp. | 2 tsp. |

*After the first kneading, add:*

|  | SMALL | MEDIUM | LARGE |
|---|---|---|---|
| Slivered almonds | ¼ cup | ⅓ cup | ½ cup |
| Mixed dried fruit, chopped | ¼ cup | ⅓ cup | ½ cup |
| Flour equivalent | 2 cups | 3 cups | 3½ cups |

**CYCLE:** sweet, basic, no timer (add fruit/nuts at beep)
**SETTING:** light to medium

# EASY HERB BREAD

Depending on the meal, use your favorite herb: basil, cilantro, oregano, mint, parsley, or a prepared mix of herbs such as Italian, Greek, etc. This bread makes a great egg strata for breakfast or brunch; leftovers can be used for croutons, or use the dried bread as a basis for bread crackers. Make the medium size recipe on the dough cycle for appetizer pockets, or Bread Bowls, page 14, or Bread Wreaths, page 15.

|  | SMALL | MEDIUM | LARGE |
|---|---|---|---|
| Water | ¾ cup | 1⅛ cups | 1¼ cups |
| Olive oil | 1½ Tbsp. | 2 Tbsp. | 3 Tbsp. |
| Sugar | 2 tsp. | 1 Tbsp. | 1½ Tbsp. |
| Salt | ½ tsp. | ¾ tsp. | 1 tsp. |
| Dried herbs | 1 Tbsp. | 1½ Tbsp. | 2 Tbsp. |
| Bread flour | 2 cups | 3 cups | 3½ cups |
| Yeast | 1 tsp. | 1½ tsp. | 2 tsp. |
| Flour equivalent | 2 cups | 3 cups | 3½ cups |

**CYCLE:** basic, timer
**SETTING:** medium

# OREGANO BREAD

This is an absolute must with spaghetti or lasagna—an often requested bread. Once you have this you'll never go back to plain old garlic bread! Several bread testers have "placed orders" for this when entertaining with Italian meals.

| | SMALL | MEDIUM | LARGE |
|---|---|---|---|
| Water | ¾ cup | 1⅛ cups | 1½ cups |
| Olive oil | 2 Tbsp. | ¼ cup | ⅓ cup |
| Parmesan cheese, grated | 3 Tbsp. | ¼ cup | ⅓ cup |
| Sugar, optional | 1 tsp. | 1½ tsp. | 2 tsp. |
| Salt | ½ tsp. | ¾ tsp. | 1 tsp. |
| Oregano, dried | 2 tsp. | 1 Tbsp. | 1½ Tbsp. |
| Bread flour | 2 cups | 3 cups | 3½ cups |
| Nonfat dry milk | 3 Tbsp. | ¼ cup | ⅓ cup |
| Yeast | 1½ tsp. | 2 tsp. | 2½ tsp. |
| Flour equivalent | 2 cups | 3 cups | 3½ cups |

**CYCLE:** basic, timer
**SETTING:** medium

Add pine nuts for an optional topping.

# GARLIC PARMESAN BREAD

If you're a garlic bread lover, this is for you. Feel free to increase or decrease the amount of garlic powder to suit your taste. Very aromatic and great, of course, with Italian meals. Make sure the garlic powder is fresh and use freshly grated Parmesan. To use fresh garlic instead of garlic powder; use 1 to 2 cloves, minced.

|  | SMALL | MEDIUM | LARGE |
| --- | --- | --- | --- |
| Water | ⅔ cup | 1 cup | 1⅛ cups |
| Margarine or butter | 2 Tbsp. | 2½ Tbsp. | 3 Tbsp. |
| Honey | 2 tsp. | 1 Tbsp. | 1½ Tbsp. |
| Parmesan cheese, grated | ½ cup | ⅔ cup | ¾ cup |
| Salt | ½ tsp. | ¾ tsp. | 1 tsp. |
| Garlic powder | 1 tsp. | 1½ tsp. | 2 tsp. |
| Bread flour | 2 cups | 3 cups | 3½ cups |
| Yeast | 1 tsp. | 1½ tsp. | 2 tsp. |
| Flour equivalent | 2 cups | 3 cups | 3½ cups |

**CYCLE:** sweet, basic, timer
**SETTING:** medium

# ANADAMA BREAD

A very different tasting bread—the molasses gives it just the right "oomph." Legend has it that a fisherman, tired of his wife's cooking, devised this recipe. As he sat down to eat, he mumbled "Anna, damn her" and from then on this was "Anadama" bread.

|  | SMALL | MEDIUM | LARGE |
| --- | --- | --- | --- |
| Water | ⅞ cup | 1 cup | 1⅛ cups |
| Molasses | 2 Tbsp. | ¼ cup | ⅓ cup |
| Margarine or butter | 1 Tbsp. | 1 Tbsp. | 1½ Tbsp. |
| Salt | ½ tsp. | ¾ tsp. | 1 tsp. |
| Yellow Cornmeal | 3 Tbsp. | ¼ cup | ⅓ cup |
| Bread flour | 2 cups | 3 cups | 3½ cups |
| Yeast | 1½ tsp. | 2 tsp. | 2½ tsp. |
| Flour equivalent | 2+ cups | 3¼ cups | 3¾ cups |

**CYCLE:** sweet, basic, timer
**SETTING:** medium

A bread machine gives the ability to make yeasted rolls, breadsticks, and more with relatively little effort. The machine does the initial kneading (the hardest part) and allows the dough to rise for the first time. When the dough is removed, it can be filled, shaped and allowed to rise a second time prior to baking in a conventional oven. See also Overnight Dough, page 14.

# DOUGH CYCLE

# BRIOCHE

MAKES 16

These make marvelous coffee rolls with a very rich texture. It's worth using butter instead of margarine. Be sure to make plenty, as people will go back for seconds and even thirds! This dough will be somewhat moist, which results in a light end product. Add only enough flour to prevent sticking, either while the machine is kneading or after the dough has been removed. To make Overnight Dough with hot brioche in the morning, see directions on page 14.

| | |
|---|---|
| 1 cup milk | 1 tsp. salt |
| 4 Tbsp. butter | 3–3½ cups bread flour |
| 2 eggs | 1½ tsp. yeast |
| 3 Tbsp. sugar | |

Remove dough from machine. Form dough into 12 large balls and 12 small balls.

Place large balls of dough a parchment-lined baking sheet. Press down in the center of each one to form an indentation into which you place a small ball of dough.

Cover and let rise for about 40 minutes. Heat oven to 375°F. Brush tops of brioche with a mixture of 1 beaten egg and 1 tablespoon sugar. Bake for 15 to 20 minutes, until golden brown.

# ALMOND BUTTER CRESCENTS

**MAKES 8**

These are extremely simple to make. To make Overnight Dough for hot crescents in the morning, see page 14.

½ cup milk
4 Tbsp. butter
1½ tsp. almond extract
2 eggs
⅓ cup sugar
½ tsp. salt

3–3¼ cups all-purpose flour
1½ tsp. yeast

*Filling:*
2 Tbsp. melted butter
1 tsp. almond extract
Glaze: 1 egg beaten with 1 Tbsp. water

On a lightly floured surface, roll dough into a large circle. Brush mixture of melted butter and almond extract over dough.

Cut circle into 8 pieces, as you would a pie. Roll each piece from wide end to tip of triangle so that it forms a crescent.

Brush each roll with glaze. Place on a cornmeal-covered baking sheet, cover and let rise for about 1 hour. Heat oven to 350°F. Bake crescents for 15 to 20 minutes, or until golden.

**ALMOND NUT CRESCENTS:** Sprinkle ¼ cup chopped almonds on top of melted butter-almond mixture before cutting the dough.

**ORANGE PRESERVE CRESCENTS:** Replace almond extract in dough with orange extract. Instead of filling, place a tablespoon of orange preserves on the wide end of the crescent. Roll each crescent so that the preserves are tightly encased. Or, use almond extract and apricot preserves.

**BRIE CRESCENTS:** With or without the almond extract in the dough and filling, brush butter on crescent. Place a slice of brie cheese on the wide end of the crescent and roll so that the cheese is tightly encased.

# CINNAMON ROLLS

MAKES 12

These rolls are very good and not overly sweet. If you want a sweeter bun, make a glaze out of milk and powdered sugar to spread over the tops while still warm. Baking these rolls in muffin cups makes them rise beautifully and look uniform. To make Overnight Dough with hot rolls in the morning, see directions on page 14.

1 cup milk
2 Tbsp. butter
1 egg
2 Tbsp. sugar
½ tsp. salt
3–3½ cups all-purpose flour
1½ tsp. yeast

*Filling:*
¼ cup sugar
1½ Tbsp. cinnamon
½ cup raisins, optional
¼ cup chopped nuts, optional
Glaze: 2 Tbsp. melted butter

Remove dough from machine. Roll dough into a rectangle, brush with melted butter and spread cinnamon mixture over butter. Roll dough as a jellyroll and cut into slices about 1½-inches thick. Place each slice in a muffin cup, cover and let rise for 35 to 40 minutes. Brush tops lightly with melted butter. Heat oven to 400°F. Bake rolls for 20 to 25 minutes.

# PARKER HOUSE DINNER ROLLS

MAKES 12

Now synonymous with American dinner rolls, these were originated by
The Parker House restaurant in Boston.

1 cup milk
2 Tbsp. margarine or butter
1 egg
1 Tbsp. sugar
½ tsp. salt

2½–3 cups all-purpose flour
2 tsp. yeast
*For brushing:* 3–4 Tbsp. melted butter
*Glaze:* 1 egg, beaten

After completion of dough cycle, knead dough by hand for about 5 minutes.
Roll out and cut with a biscuit cutter (or cup). Brush with melted butter. Fold
circles in half and place, fold side down, in buttered muffin tins. Cover and let
rise for 35 to 45 minutes. Heat oven to 350°F. Brush tops of rolls with glaze and
bake for 20 to 25 minutes.

# SWEET ROLLS

MAKES 12

These are wonderful topped with jam. A special treat. To make Overnight Dough with hot rolls in the morning, see directions on page 14. You can also easily make them into wreaths, which make a great gift idea.

¾ cup milk

4 Tbsp. margarine or butter

1 egg

¼ cup sugar

1 tsp. salt

3 cups all-purpose flour

2 tsp. yeast

Confectioners' sugar, optional for dusting

After completion of dough cycle, shape dough into 12 balls and place in muffin cups. Cover and let rise for 45 to 60 minutes. Heat oven to 350°F. If desired, brush top of dough with additional melted butter just before baking. Bake rolls for 15 to 20 minutes or until done. Sift confectioners' sugar over the rolls before serving.

# CHALLAH

Challah is a very light and wonderful tasting bread. The dough is somewhat moist, and you should add only enough flour to prevent sticking, either while the machine is kneading or after the dough has been removed.

⅔ cup water
2 eggs
2 Tbsp. vegetable oil
2 Tbsp. sugar
1 tsp. salt

3–3¼ cups bread flour
1½ tsp. yeast
*Glaze:* 1 egg, beaten
1–2 Tbsp. poppy or sesame seeds, optional

Remove dough from machine and divide into 3 pieces; roll each piece into a rope about 14 inches long and braid on a greased baking sheet. Cover and let rise for about 45 minutes. Heat oven to 350°F. Brush top of dough with egg glaze and sprinkle with seeds, if using. Bake for 45 minutes.

# HAMBURGER/HOT DOG ROLLS

MAKES 12

These are the best. Make plenty and freeze the extras for the next time, if you have any left, that is! Wonderful as is, but good with variations as well. Not only are these great for burgers and dogs, but for sandwiches too.

1 cup water
2 Tbsp. margarine or butter
2 Tbsp. sugar
2 tsp. salt

3–3¼ cups bread flour
3 Tbsp. nonfat dry milk
2 tsp. yeast

Remove dough from machine. Punch it down and let it rest for 20 minutes. Form into 12 balls, make bun shapes and flatten. Cover and let rise for 1 hour. Heat oven to 375°F. Bake rolls for 15 to 20 minutes or until golden.

VARIATIONS: Add 1½ tablespoons sesame seeds, poppy seeds, chives, or minced onion to the dough. Brush the tops of the buns with a beaten egg and sprinkle with sesame seeds immediately prior to baking.

# HOT CROSS BUNS

MAKES 12

You needn't wait for Easter to come around to enjoy these —with or without the frosting cross. Absolutely delicious.

¾ cup milk
2 eggs
3 Tbsp. margarine or butter
¼ cup sugar
½ tsp. salt
1 tsp. cinnamon
3–3¼ cups all-purpose flour
1½ tsp. yeast

*Add at end of kneading:* ¾ cup raisins

*Glaze:* egg yolk mixed with 2 tsp. water

*Frosting:*
1 cup confectioners' sugar
½ tsp. vanilla extract
1 Tbsp. milk

About 5 minutes prior to the end of machine kneading, add raisins, or knead them in by hand at the completion of the cycle. After a short kneading, let dough rest for about 10 minutes. Cut dough into 12 pieces, shape each into a ball and place in a greased baking dish. Cover and let rise about 35 minutes or until doubled in bulk. Brush with glaze. Heat oven to 350°F. Bake buns for 20 to 25 minutes.

If desired, after buns are completely cool, mix frosting ingredients and drizzle in the shape of a cross.

# PITA BREAD

MAKES 10

The very hot oven makes these breads puff up during baking. Well worth the few minutes involved to make. Easy to have done in time for lunch sandwiches.

1⅓ cups water
3 Tbsp. olive oil
1½ Tbsp. sugar
1 tsp. salt

2 cups bread flour
1½ cups whole wheat flour
2 tsp. yeast.

Upon completion of the dough cycle, divide dough into 10 pieces and roll into balls. Flatten each ball into a disk, rolling each one into a circle of about 6 inches. Place on a baking sheet. Heat oven to 500°F. Let dough rise for about 20 minutes and bake for 8 to 10 minutes.

# CRUSTY PIZZA DOUGH

This recipe makes 2 large 15-inch pizzas or 3 medium 10-inch pizzas. See below for ideas for toppings.

1⅓ cups water
2 Tbsp. olive oil
1 Tbsp. sugar

½ tsp. salt
4 cups bread flour
1½ tsp. yeast

Remove dough from machine and roll into 2 or 3 rectangles or circles, depending on the pan to be used. Place on greased pan. Heat oven to 500°F. If you want a thicker crust, cover and let rise about 30 minutes. If you want a thin crust, top immediately with sauce, cheese and other desired toppings (don't forget herbs). Bake for about 10 minutes, until crust is brown and cheese is melted.

**SUGGESTED TOPPINGS:** Basic pizza sauce, mozzarella, basil and/or oregano, any meat or vegetable topping. Salsa instead of pizza sauce, black beans, corn, mozzarella, and pepper jack cheeses. Cocktail sauce instead of pizza sauce, cooked and diced shrimp, mozzarella with or without feta and mint.

# ENGLISH MUFFINS

MAKES 12–15

This is a soft dough. To have dough ready in the morning, see the Overnight Dough section on page 14.

| | |
|---|---|
| 1 cup water or milk | ½ tsp. salt |
| 2 Tbsp. butter or margarine | 3 cups all-purpose flour |
| 1 egg | 1½ tsp. rapid or quick yeast |
| 1 Tbsp. sugar | |

Remove dough from machine upon completion of dough cycle. Press dough by hand into a ½-inch thick rectangle on a cornmeal-covered surface. Turn dough over several times so that both sides are coated with cornmeal to prevent sticking.

Cut muffins with a biscuit or cookie cutter or use the top of a glass. Place on a lightly greased baking sheet, cover and let rise for 45 to 60 minutes.

Cook on an ungreased griddle or cast-iron skillet over low to medium heat for 5 to 7 minutes on each side until golden brown. Cook muffins fairly close together—leaving only a half-inch or so in between. Split open with a fork and serve warm or toasted.

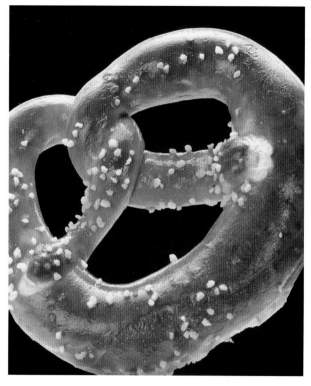

# PRETZELS

MAKES 15–24

I bet you can't eat just one! Make these treats any size you like.

1⅓ cups water
2 Tbsp. margarine or butter
1½ Tbsp. sugar
¾ tsp. salt
4 cups all-purpose flour
2½ tsp. yeast

*For boiling:*
4 cups water
1½ Tbsp. baking soda

Cut dough into short strips, roll into ropes and shape into pretzels. Cover and let rise on a greased baking sheet for about 45 minutes. Heat oven to 475°F.

In a cast iron or other nonaluminum pan, bring water and baking soda to a simmer. Gently lower (by hand or slotted spoon) pretzels into water and cook about 1 minute, turning once. Do not let water come to a full boil. Remove pretzels and return to greased baking sheet. Sprinkle with coarse salt or kosher salt. Bake for about 12 minutes.

# INDEX